This book is dedicated to

*"All the Adherents of the **Buffalo Cult!**"*

Author,

Gautham S

Kumbakonam, Tamil Nadu

Pothuraju, the Buffalo King

POTHURAJU, A Calumniated Pre-Vedic Deity

Author & Publisher: **GAUTHAM S** {Kumbakonam, Tamil Nadu, INDIA}

Cover Design by: **GAUTHAM S**

Edited & Interior Design: **BRIKUT A**

ISBN: **978-93-342-2655-3**

First Edition: **05 February 2025**

For information, email **brkuti@gmail.com**

This book is dedicated to "All the Adherents of the ***Buffalo Cult***!"

Preface

By the decree of God, I present you this book, which is a result of various studies by historians, which helped me brew a concoction based on all their research and also not forgetting the 'people' who served as sources of lost folklores. A conglomeration of all these reports, shook my religious beliefs. I do not intend to offend any person or religion in this endeavor.

I hear by share this book, for the young and elderly, eager to understand and witness the changes that occurs by time, leading us to an uncertain destination.

Contents

INTRODUCTION

This research is about how, very few Pre-Vedic deities multiply themselves into various sects, cults and forms in accordance to the locations and native names as their key of acceptance. Though their shrines are now sanskritized and magnificent, these deities were once accessible to common man and their back stories simple. Until the Vedic Gods made their way through the Puranas, turning all the Tutelary Deities into Demi-Gods, who were classified as those who serve the supreme Puranic Gods.

There are historians and scholars who are putting out the facts of these Pre-Vedic deities and their survival, a result of the struggles their devotees went through.

»

In a country like India that's culturally diverse, there is always a battle amongst castes and races to prove themselves the cream of the society.

The haughty sects are those who won this battle, either by strength or "by any means necessary". Though survival becomes secondary, holding the higher status is always envisioned as a sign of respect by human race.

Things get dark, when "hunt for hunger" becomes "hunting for sport". When the remnants decay, the picture never looks pleasant. Unfortunately, this is what happens during the process of maintaining the higher stature in society. Falling prey to this battle are cultures and deities of those under.

One such deity is the topic of discussion recently.

A HUNT

A hunt for what's lost. A pastoral deity who has various names in various regions. Stories of this deity has too many versions depending on the cultural exchanges, native languages and a hint of imagination in folklores.

Few of this deity's names are:

- ***Mhasoba/ Mhaskoba/ Mhatoba***
- ***Pothuraju/ Pothiraja***
- ***Karuppu***
- ***Sudalai Maadan***
- ***Vishnu Maya/ Sathan Swamy***
- ***Mula Maysondayya/ Maisonday***
- ***Bhootharaja***
- ***Uramma and Marikambe – Buffalo/ Emme***
- ***Betal/ Vetal***
- ***Gorla***
- ***Mahisasura***
- ***Yamantaka/ Vajra-Bhairav***

He is considered as the deity of the ignoble compared to the Puranic or Vedic deities. The topic is too vast to comprehend, hence we are going to take this step by step for easier understanding.

In this, there are numerous stories associated with each name of the same deity. There was once a period where nomads, tribes of various kind and diverse cults walked on this land. They coexisted without having to prove the superiority of their deities and belief systems.

These deities never needed an 'invoking process' nor any rules or rituals for installation. While the Aryans believed that an idol needed to be given its first breath through Sanskrit hymns by the Brahmin priests. They also believe till date, that through Mantras and rituals, an idol or the divine itself can be purified. This very idea of the Aryans is grotesque. They firmly believe that God is obliged to Sanskrit hymns and abide by the Brahmin rituals, whereas the pre-vedic deities are believed to be unbound and independent. Every man that walked on this very land had a deity associated with him or his bloodline, and these deities were believed to be the benevolent spirits of their ancestors, who would protect them when they surrendered themselves. Now, let's go through the theology of Deccan deities, with different versions of each/ same.

Chapter 1:

MHASOBA

First of the most misinterpreted **pre-vedic deity**, which was later absorbed into puranas and portrayed as the most unpleasant entity.

The Name "MHAS/ MHASO" originates from "MAHIS" (buffalo) which later becomes Mahish/ Mahisha, "BA" - a word used to address someone respectfully.

Though there are numerous temples for Mhasoba all over Maharastra, India, there are no background stories of the Deity's origin. But in Maharastra, He is considered to be one of the most popular deity among certain clans. He also has a lot of folk stories.

Mhasoba idol at Mhasoba Temple

In the land of the Maratha, it is thought that the birthplace of Mhasoba is Kharwade, Pune. In the 13th century, Bauji had a vision of Mhasoba's birth or existence in the present place of the Temple of Mhasoba. It's a **400-year-old temple** as mentioned by the temple administration. Yet, it is classified as a 'B Class' pilgrimage.

He is a **Kshetrapal/ Grama Devata**, who accepts animal sacrifices. Since He is a kshetrapal, He is often associated with Khandoba or Bhairav. He is the deity of Pastoral, Agricultural and Shephard communities. He accepts alcohol, meat or anything offered with love by His devotees. He prefers to stay in robust environments, open-to-sky on an elevated platform or mountains. Later walks down the hill and interacts with rustic deities who reside in the lap-lands or villages nearby.

His story says: He travelled from the **Konkan region** all the way to Pune - MH, He reaches a mountain top or a hilltop in Hinjewadi, Pune. Accompanied by **Hirai and Sitai**, the twin sisters. He then requests one of His devotees to take Him down the hill and leave Him near river 'Mula'. Thereby landing in Wakad, Pune, where He was smitten by **Jogubai**'s beauty. They fall in love and marry. Every year on Chaitra Pournami day, a palanquin is carried from Hinjewadi to Wakad marking the marriage of Mhasoba and Jogubai.

Later it is seen that Jogubai objects the company of Hirai and Sitai. Here is where the folk stories and folk songs bring in their flavors of imagination by providing various reasons, as to why Jogubai envied their company. Later, Mhasoba decides to drown the sisters in Mula River. This incident is witnessed by a fisherman and a washer man. It is said that the sisters' corpses float on the opposite banks of river Mula where a shrine for them still exist. The body of the fisherman and the washer man who were killed by Mhasoba while they witnessed the sisters being murdered, floated near Hinjewadi. There are so many other incidents that is said to have occurred, like Mhasoba along with this wife Jogubai visits His elder sister near Kothrud, Pune. An annual event is observed at the **Tukai Devi**

temple where she welcomes her brother and sister-in-law, which again signifies the harvest season of farmers.

He is often associated with the demon god 'VETAL' by the **Dhangar community**. In the Konkan region, He is seen as Vetal-baba. Mhasoba is a pre-vedic deity with no protocols for worshipping. He is more friendly and accessible. He is a tantric deity who always accompanies the Seven Sisters called 'SATI ASARAS'.

The Sati Asaras, who are misunderstood for Apsaras because of their association with 'AP' – water. They are called Sapta Kanni (in the Delta Regions), Saath Saheli or Behne (in North), Saptha Mathrika, Yelu Kannimargal and more.

Mhasoba is often seen as their guardian, brother in some areas, companion in a few. Hence there is no specific relationship mentioned anywhere. However, the majority of people believe Him to be a guardian of these seven sisters.

Mhasoba with Sati-Asaras

Initially Mhasoba or the Sati Asaras had no proper idols or sculptures. As they were worshipped by nomads, tribes and shepherds who constantly moved around with their herd. Hence, they had no specific shape, (but in recent times, a Buffalo shaped metal head is being installed). The shepherds placed '8' stones on a podium or platform, where the biggest stone being Mhasoba and the remaining, the 7-sisters. Usually, these stones are decorated with turmeric paste and flowers. During night, things like alcohol, meat and cigars are being placed in front of their deity and the group rests alongside hoping their Kshetrapal would protect them and their herd, at night, in the wild, from animals and ghastly spirits.

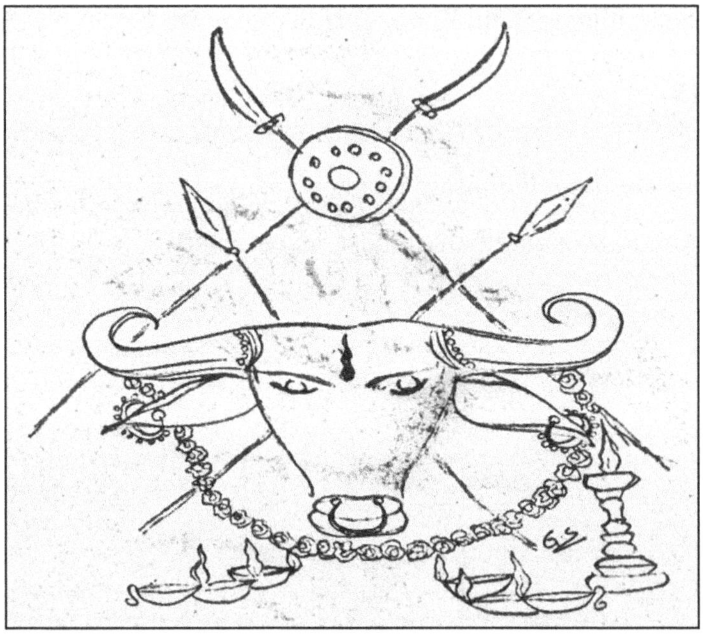

Buffalo head mask - worshipped at Mhasoba temple

1.1 AFTER BEING ABSORBED INTO PURANAS

Puranic Status:

This rustic, unrefined tantric deity becomes Mahisasura who is slayed by 'Durga'. Puranas convey the ideology of Aryans' superiority over these pre-vedic deities. Even now, some of these pre-vedic deities are non-brahminical temples, where sacrifices are still being practiced, and all these tantric deities are classified under Atharvana Veda. The Puranas are being altered and extended from time to time as we all see. When failed attempts of eliminating these Deccan Deities, they have been accepted as forms of 'Shiva' during the augmentation process.

Mhasoba or Mhatoba in Telugu states: **The POTHURAJU**.

Chapter 2:

POTHURAJU

Pothuraju's most common form among the adherents

The migrating shepherds and cowherds are seen moving around the subcontinent in every direction, in search of food and pastoral land for grazing.

When this bunch entered the Telugu region, 'Mhasoba' became 'POTHURAJU'. The literal translation of "POTHU" is Buffalo or Cattle and "RAJU" means King. Here He becomes the KING OF BUFFALOES. He again is addressed as Pothuraju, Pothurayudu, Pothulayya, Pothulingudu etc. Again the name Pothulingudu signifies the idea, of being adopted by the **Shaivaites**.

Pothuraju guarding Seven Sisters

In Andhra Pradesh and Telangana, He is the guardian deity of the Seven (7) Sisters, here the number of goddesses varies like seven (7), forty-nine (49), ninety-nine (99), hundred-and-one or hundred-and-eight etc. The number of sister goddesses usually vary according to regions.

Pothuraju worshipped in a wooden/ stone staff, in various forms

He is a guardian of these village Goddesses, sometimes times their brother, who wards off the evil in the village. He walks ahead of these Goddesses protecting them. Sometimes He is seen alone without any Goddesses to accompany. He alone becomes the Kshetrapal or the Grama-Devata. In the Maratha region, it's a formless stone used for worship, but in Andhra & Telangana 'A Twin Sticks/ Poles/ Pillar-like-stones/ 2-lingam shaped structures are installed on the ground and worshipped as POTHURAJU. It is said that these 2-sticks or lingams represent the Horns of a Buffalo. This could have been something, which the tribe may have picked while migrating to new lands.

When he is with multiple Goddesses, He's in a corner and when He's with one Goddess, He stands right in front of her, to keep a watch on her at all times. Just like supervising and keeping her protected, like a concerned brother, and sometimes beside her as a consort or companion.

There is a story in Andhra Pradesh, that says the brother of ANKAMMA i.e., Pothularaju, was not offered anything for quite a long time and this increased His hunger. This enraged Ankamma, who warns the villagers about unleashing a famine. They immediately sacrificed Buffaloes, Goats, Poultry etc. and the head of the buffaloes were kept on either sides of His idol. The feast ended by offering unbroken or un-cracked whole coconuts, tamarind rice, alcohol and new clothes. The main deity Ankamma is still deprived of all these offerings, as the priests banned meat offerings to the Goddess. Such practices of offering **satvik food** spread to all the temples of female deities, as a result of which the idols of Pothuraju were moved outside the temple. Banning meat was seen as a sign of purity and attaining higher stature. In Telangana, Ankamma/ Yellamma or Maha Kali in some cases, Pothuraju is seen walking in front of or alongside the '**Bonalu**', a divine offering to the female deity or His sister. This practice or act is an epitome of a concerned brother about His hungry sister.

In some temples, it is very difficult to identify Pothuraju's existence in the temple premises. It is because a 6-inch or 8-inch pole or lingam-like structure is installed on a podium, which looks like a penis, right in front of the Goddess. When a non-Brahmin priest is asked about that, he informs that, it's the very first Pothuraju's form that was installed when the female deity's temple was erected.

Pothuraju - Human form carved on a wooden/ stone pillar

Now a days, the stones or the twin pillars or twin lingams-like structure are taking human forms. They are being replaced by stone sculptures where a male figure holds – sword, whip, sickle, bowl of turmeric, skull, slayed head, club, shield etc. and in some cases lion. Usually, a mix and match of any of these. We can see that, very old temples of Pothuraju like '**Kalyanapu Lovu**, Andhra Pradesh', a Shiva Lingam is being treated as Pothuraju. These changes may have occurred because of the availability of stone sculptors. Also, as a part of development, a formless deity gains a form. Although these idols can make the devotees feel more emotionally connected to the deity, these changes could have been a result of cultural exchanges in the recent times.

2.1 STORY IN THE LAND OF TELUGU

Pothuraju - Stone sculpture with human form, open-to-sky

Pothuraju attained a Puranic status among the Telugu crowd, as the entire region was sanskritized, the culture and language of the existing tribes in these regions were influenced.

He is said to be or seen as an avatar of Vishnu. A Vaishnava cult story describes how Rama and Sita had a petty fight during a sport in their exile. Sita invites Rama for a rematch or in some versions she challenges Rama for a different sport, but then Rama denies, due to lack of interest.

This enrages Sita and ends up cursing Rama that in his forthcoming avatar, he would be surrounded by wicked men. Rama in turn curses Sita saying, she would be born as **KAMAVALLI** and she would laugh/ smile every time she heard his name. Although, Kamavalli does not have a significant position in any of Pothiraju's temples, instead some locals consider one out of the twin structure that represents Pothuraju to be Kamavalli, his consort.

Although there are no such mentions about this story in Valmiki Ramayana. Hence, these can be folklores that may have sprouted from the imagination of the natives while shoving a local deity into the puranas. There would have been no objections for contaminating the Original Idea of POTHURAJU, as people would have felt that this would in turn glorify their deity.

The story continues that, Shiva placed the energy of Lakshmi in a pond. When Parvati was parched, she consumed seven (7) gulps of water from this pond, creating the seven Goddesses. Later Shiva and Parvati could not take care of these seven Goddesses and hence they created Pothuraju from the eldest sister's energy to guard them. That is the reason for people to believe that He is the embodiment of His elder sister Gangamma/ Yellamma. Brahma created triplets out of this pond, and Pothuraju took Kamavalli, one among triplets to be His wife.

In some accounts, He is a guardian deity who blocks evil spirits and diseases from entering the village. In a village called Kesavaram, Andhra Pradesh, there were accounts of Him guiding the villagers who lost their way, sometimes he holds a flame-beau or a flame-torch at nights, blessing the travelers en route who are too scared of the dark. In Andhra Pradesh and Telangana, He is not seen as Tantric deity, instead He is a guardian, who demands sacrifices, meat, alcohol, cigars etc. Here He whips His devotees, curing their ailments, eliminating the evil aura, blessing the devotees with prosperity etc.

This idea of whiplashes should have been espoused from the concept of 'Kadak Lakshmi' from the Maharastran tribes, where the Pothuraju tribe whip themselves walking in front of 'Kadak Lakshmi', a deity carried in a basket by women. Kadak Lakshmi – the very strict elder sister of Lakshmi who punishes impartially, hence the name 'Kadak'. He is seen as an embodiment of Kadak Lakshmi i.e. Yellamma. He clears way for her by walking in front of her. This self-punishing act without a reason, should have been a later development of customs by their clans. Although this action of whipping themselves and others can be commonly found in Betal - Goa, Soma-Kunitha and Bhootakunitha – Karnataka, Saattai-Adi and Perambu-Adi by Karuppu – Tamil Nadu, Bhootaraja Cult etc.

There are more folklores associated with Him. Folklores cannot be ignored just for the reason of not being documented as a transcript. Sometimes the folklores are seen to have stuck to the 'Original' and are more reliable sources. As we can observe that these 'left-out deities', in the later period of the puranic era did not lose its followers. Hence when they were absorbed into the puranas, all the male deities were either associated with Shiva or Vishnu and all the female deities with Parvati or Lakshmi. A status upgrade is given to these rustic deities and was accepted by their followers, as their deities were glorified. But they never realized the fact of their roots being sabotaged.

The migrating Telugu shepherds/ Yadavas or the Kamma or the Kapu community during the NAYAKAR/ NAICKER regime, moved further down south. Thus introducing this deity to the new Nayakar/ Naicker territories and northern parts of Tamil Nadu. There is another story of 'KATAMARAJU', another pastoral deity who sought blessings of Pothuraju before migrating or waging a battle. Hence, when these Yadava communities migrated to Tamil Nadu, they brought-in Pothuraju as well as Katamaraju as their Tutelary deities. However, there was a parallel existence of the same deity in a different name in the 'KONGU BELT' and dry regions like Madurai, Dindigul etc. The people in these areas called Him "KARUPPU", literally translates to Black.

Eventually the Pothuraju cult was accepted in Tamil Nadu during the **Pallavas rule**, who were hiring narrators of **Bharata Puranam** to keep up the high spirits of their soldiers. A new deity (Pothuraju) was included as a part of Draupadi pantheon. Including new deities into a newly developing pantheon was not new. All it needed was a story to connect with the most superior deity of the pantheon or around which the story was developed.

2.2 STORIES IN THE LAND OF TAMIZH

As the deity made its way into the land of Tamils, He took the form of '**nadukkal**' (similar to '**veergal**' in Karnataka and Maharastra) initially, meaning hero-stone. Later when He found a spot for Himself, He was given a bas-relief structure and wooden idols. During this period, He gets a shape from a shapeless or pole-like structure, to a human-like sculpture and lingam form.

2.2.1 According to few authors who studied the Draupadi pantheon, the story about Pothuraju is:

'Sunita', the descendent of Pandavas, grandson of Janamejaya relocates his kingdom to now-called Gingee, Tamil Nadu. He is seen constantly threatened by Rochaka, a demonic force. Rochaka had a boon of thousand heads emerging every time his head was slayed. The boon of thousand heads could have been an exaggeration, to describe the severity of his cruelty and strength. However, if his final/ 1000th head fell to the ground, the slayer would die immediately, bringing Rochaka back to life.

Worried king Sunita sought advice from a few learned Brahmins, who suggested invoking one of his ancestor's, Goddess Draupadi, who was Kali Herself and seek her help. Once that was successful, she orders him to bring Pothiraja, the **King of Virata**, who was then residing in the eternally burning sacrificial fire somewhere in Kalinga region (the northern coast of Andhra Pradesh and Odisha). She felt He was the only person who could assist her fighting this demon, also catch his final head before touching the ground.

When king Sunita reached Kalinga, it is said that Pothiraja emerged out of sacrificial altar along with five (5) divine weapons that Draupadi would need for the battle. Even today, Pothiraja idols are seen holding the 1000th head in one hand and a sword in other. Since then, the '**muthal-maryadai**' i.e., Pooja offerings and respects are first dedicated to Pothiraja in all the Draupadi temples, even today. During the time of the annual celebrations, Draupadi_and Pothuraju are both the recipients of Buffalo sacrifices but, the practice now is brought to an end.

About less than 0.2 KM from the Gingee temple, there is the 'thee-panjan-kovil', adjacent to it is the temple of King Sunita, where he was cremated. However, the sati who entered the pyre was Sunita's concubine, a Telugu speaking Naidu for whose lineage he left all his provisions. Since his wife failed to immolate herself for her husband.

The **Konars, Velalars, Pillais, Muthaliars, Vanniars** and a **few Brahmin** communities claim their lineage of these deities in Gingee (Tamil Nadu). Hence, the five divine weapons like "**Veera Jaattai, Veera Kantham/ Bandara Petti, Veera Kadhgam, Kunthayutham and Silambu**" are shared among themselves as symbols that represent these communities.

This story is recited only in the northern dry mountain areas of Tamil Nadu. There are variants of this story according to different communities. The same deity has another version of story when He enters the borders of Tamil Nadu and Karnataka. This version is widespread among the **Thigala** community, who claim to be **Tamil Vanniars**.

There is one significant mutation of this deity, during this phase. He is accepted in the Draupadi pantheon as the '**Veera Bhadra of Kurukshetra**' maybe because He has a sword and decapitated head in his hands similar to Veera Bhadra's appearance. The narrators of '**Bharata Koothu**' also calls Him '**Pormannan Veera Bhadran**', '**Ugra Bhadran**', as there were already many stories of Pothiraja that He was an avatar of Siva or Siva's son. This widespread confusion caused an impact on the 7-sisters concept.

Ideology of Veera Bhadhra along with Sapta-Kanyas

People started installing Veera Bhadra with the 'Saptha Kannis' or 'Sati Asaras'. Thus, usurping the position of shapeless Mhasoba or the veergal Pothuraju. Although there are few other reasons like – adopting 'Saptha Kanyas' into the 'SHAKTH MATH', which later became a part of 'SHAIVA MATH', Veera Bhadra of Shaiva Math seemed more appropriate than MHASOBA or POTHURAJU to the Shaivaites. Even today, there are many Draupadi temples that have replaced Pothiraja with Veera Bhadra to glorify the status of Draupadi, thus considering her as an avatar of Parvati.

2.2.2 The second story – **'Elu Suttina Kote'**. This story is widely accepted in Karnataka, Thiruvannamalai - TN and Krishnagiri – TN, to be the origin of Pothiraja and is passed as an oral tradition.

In a place called '**Sivanandapuri - TN**', it is said that Parvati and Siva decide to spend some time alone together, away from Kailasa. Parvati designs and builds a sandcastle with seven layered walls, in which Siva places a few divine weapons. But, there was a problem that the couple realized later, that is, if these weapons were moved from their place, the sandcastle might collapse. They decide to create a warrior to safeguard the sandcastle, his name was Pothiraja, King of Buffaloes, the guy who is a recipient of whole coconuts (not broken). He is also provided with hundreds of soldiers to assist him, by Siva to safeguard the castle.

During the time of **Kurukshetra**, the Pandavas were in need of divine and powerful weapons to win the war. Krishna suggests that Arjuna and himself should try stealing the divine weapons of Pothiraja, the then King of Sivanandapuri. They both dress up as women, Krishna as a grandmother of Arjuna, trying to sell bangles, reached the castle and rested their backs on the walls of the castle which resulted in a part of the castle getting damaged. This incident was brought to the notice of Pothiraja by His men. Enraged Pothiraja, captured them both. Bewitched by Arjuna's beauty, when produced in His court, He proposed Arjuna to become His queen. Later He gets furious, learning the fact that He was tricked by Krishna and Arjuna.

Krishna is said to have calmed Him down by offering 'Sanguvati', Arjuna's sister to marry Him, but in turn He had to grant them the weapons and participate in the war by the side of Pandavas. The birth of Sanguvati is not mentioned anywhere, nor about her marriage with Pothuraju anywhere in the Mahabharata. Finally, the war ends, granting the primal respect and offerings to Pothiraja in all the Pandavas or Draupadi temples, as a token of their gratitude.

Here, we see that Pothuraju was initially appointed to safeguard the weapons of Siva. Instead, He gives them away to Krishna, failing the purpose of His birth. Again, a character named 'Sanguvati', a sister of Pandavas, could have been a recent appendage to the story. This edition was done to bring Pothuraju under the cult of Draupadi. 'Sanguvati-Pothiraja thirumanam' is a play performed in Draupadi temples of Tamil Nadu.

There is a small folklore, that is a continuation of this story at the borders of Karnataka, Andhra Pradesh and Telangana, in places like Anantapur, Dharmavaram etc. that, He rested in a village near Anantapur after the Kurukshetra war to graze His herd. Here he was called POTHULAYYA. Now, it has become a Siva temple, because of the error in name change i.e., POTHULINGA or maybe the shape of the deity that resembles lingam. This could have been a misunderstanding for associating Him with Siva.

When the **NAYAK/ NAICKER/ NAYAKAR** population established their kingdoms in Madurai, Dindigul, Virudhanagar areas, they carried their Kula Devatas like Gangamma, Ankamma, Angalamma, Yellamma etc. along with Pothuraju idols. They built temples for these deities in their new lands. In some instances, they carried stones (in the shape of veergal or nadukkal) and pouches filled with mud from their tutelary (deities) temples, and installed them in their new settlements.

New temples were later built around these deities, with new fascinating stories, stories that also connected the already preceding deity of their new settlements. But, there were few things that remained unchanged, thus guarding the originality of these deities to an extent.

In districts like Virudhunagar, Pothiraja temples can be found in every few kilometers that belong to the Telugu speaking communities each having a story of their own. Sometimes, the deity refused to move from the ground it was placed while resting en route. In some cases, the deity walks along with them, points a place or a resting stone, guides His or Her people about the Dos and Don'ts of the Pooja process through an Oracle.

In one such place at the border of Thenkasi and Kerala reserve forest, the Yadava community worshipped an anthill, in which Pothiraja was believed to be residing, until a person who belonged to a higher community destroyed the anthill and asked them to leave. After this incident, it is said Pothiraja, unable to bear this insult, wandered looking for a land where He would be treated with respect. He then informs His devotees through an Oracle (Saami-Aadi) that He has now settled in a place near Devipattinam – TN, where the Palm Tree is entwined by a Neem Tree. SO, a temple is erected in honor of Pothiraja there and His devotees relocate to this new land.

As the cult of Pothuraju entered Tamil Nadu, crossed the delta regions and moved further south towards Sivagangai, Dindugal etc. A fiercely deity called KARUPPU, was cardinal. He was none other than Pothiraja Himself. Ironically, in some places, both the deities exist in the same temple complex, representing them as two different persona.

Chapter 3:

KARUPPU

KARUPPU/ KARUPPUSAMY is a complex perplexing topic – to simplify the idea of Karuppu, we must understand the concept of two different variations known so far.

Karuppu – most common form in Tamil Nadu

First – Karuppu, the primordial one that actually traces back to Pothiraja cult.

Secondly – Karuppu, warrior men who lost their lives for a noble cause, sacrifice, trying to guard an '**Ajivika**' guru or death by aspersion. This category includes various deities with a prefix of the weapons of their expertise or by locations, granting them all with the common title 'Karuppu'. As Karuppu was a term or a recognition for those who were guards. This category also includes a few 'Puli-Kutti-Kal Deities', a hero who martyred trying to save his herd from wild animals.

Meanwhile, there are deities with names that are a combination of names such as Pothi or Pothiraja, Karuppu, Sudalai, Veeran, Saathan etc. Some deities may have names that have a prefix or suffix of each other's names like Pothi-Veeran, Sudalai-Veeran, Pothi-Karuppu, Veera-Sudalai-Pothi, Maada-Karuppu, Aingulathu-Veera-Pothi etc. and the list goes on. While Pothi-Sastha, Veera-Sastha are deities where 'Sastha' is a term used by people (from Karaikudi - TN area extending up to Kanyakumari and Kerala) to address a respectful person. After the demise of a very respectful person or a selfless martyr, he would be given a position of a guardian deity as Saathan/ Sasthan in these areas. This confusion in mix-n-match of names may have occurred when the deities' purpose was confused with their names, as they were commonly categorized as guardian deities.

The primordial Karuppu's other names such as 'MAADAN' or 'SATHAN', in the Malayalam land, spread through His tales to Tamil Nadu, ending up having 'MAADAN' or 'SUDALA MAADAN' temples. But the prime concept of all these deities' links to Mhasoba or Pothuraju (just for better understanding). Eventually, these deities ended up having different folklores of their own and stood independent losing their connection with each other.

3.1 THE PRIMORDIAL KARUPPU -

3.1.1 Story 1: When Sita was abandoned by Rama, in the hermitage of Valmiki, it is said that her only-son Lava goes missing. Scared Valmiki, who was answerable, creates another boy using Kusha grass, magically. This new child had to take the place of Lava. Later, Sita is seen walking with Lava into the ashram. Shocked to see another boy, a doppelganger of her son, she draws a line and asks them to crossover. In some versions, a trial by fire, to determine the real son of Rama. This newly created boy of Valmiki is scorched, giving him a darker complexion. Hence the name Karuppu/ Black. Later the singed boy requests Sita to accept him as her child, although this is not mentioned in Valmiki Ramayana, just passed on through oral traditions. The original version says Sita gave birth to twins, one resembling her and the darker one resembling Rama. Rama decides to attain Moksha through 'Jala Samadhi', he then plans for a coronation ceremony for his sons Lava & Kusha. It is said that Lava ruled his empire with 'Lavapuri' (the modern day Lahore) as the capital of his kingdom. There is a speculation about the capital of Lava with another placed called 'Shravasthi'. Kusha rules his empire 'Kushavati', also called 'Kush-Kshetra' with Srinagar as his capital that extended from Kashmir to Indus River. This proves that Kusha ruled Kashmir, ruling out the chances of being Karuppusamy in the Southern part of Tamil Nadu. Although, there are mentions of Lava-Kusha visiting South (Koyembedu, Chennai) and initiated the notion of Pradosha-Pooja.

3.1.2 Story 2: Veera Bhadra and Kali after Daksha's head being slayed during Daksha yagna, a son is born of their union. He resides in graveyards, after few eons he is sent to Ayyanar/ Ayyapan (Siva's son) by Siva, to serve and protect him. In turn, He would be offered meat, alcohol and cigars.

In another version, He is castaway in a box by a Brahmin priest, He then reaches a village (Marnadu) in Madurai and resides in an anthill. To this day, people worship the anthill and a temple is built for Him.

3.1.3 Story 3: There is another interesting version where Parvati walks out on her husband over a petty fight, Karuppu follows her like a mama's boy. He could not live without His mother's presence and stood very close to her, facing her at all times. Noticing how clung and devoted He was to His mother, Parvati and all the forms of village Goddesses who are associated with Parvati, will have a Karuppu idol in front of them.

It is said that there are 11, 51, 101, 108 etc. types of Karuppusamy. His wives also vary from place to place like **Pechi, Pidari, Karuppi, Karuppayi and Periyayi** etc. Though all these topics are still a topic of debate, we must understand that the primordial Karuppu is Pothiraja or Mhasoba himself. Starting from Andhra, Telangana, Tamil Nadu, parts of Odisha and parts of Karnataka, always (a Goddess) a pre-vedic deity will have a Pothiraja in front of her. He will be the first to encounter, before approaching a village Goddess. Buffaloes, goats, fowls etc. were sacrificed, where the heads of these animals were kept at the foot of Pothiraja and the cooked meat were served for both the deities. Although these practices have been banned recently by the Brahmin priests, there are still few temples which follow these customs. So, there was a widespread confusion about these ferocious guardians that stood in front of the village Goddesses versus those at the gates guarding Ayyapan/ Ayyanar. Recently we can observe that Karuppu, Ayyappa and Goddesses (of any form), all these co-exist in the same temple. This could have been the influence of folklores connecting these deities and the growing popularity of these deities.

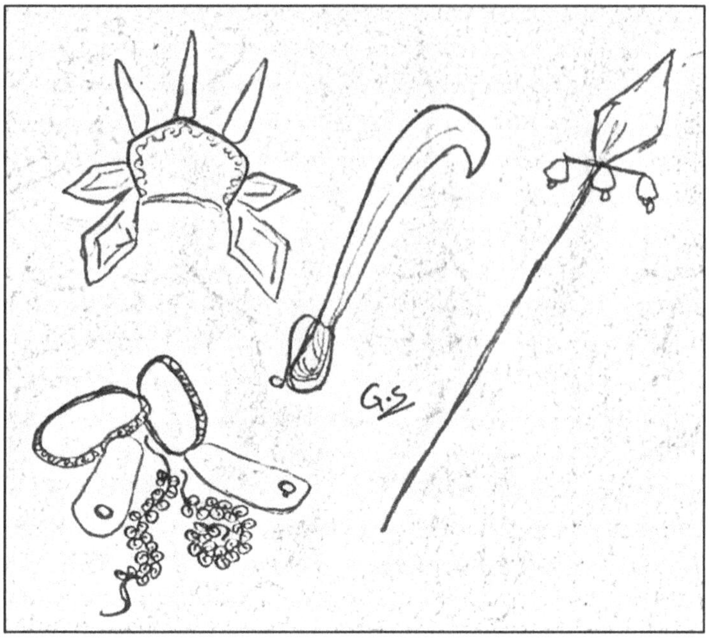

Ornaments of Karuppu worn by Oracles

It is to note that initially the 'Sami-Aadi' of Karuppusamy wore a black dress, ornaments, lit cigars and were intoxicated, they also wore a black dhoti, wore a black cap with horns and ears that resembles a buffalo, these Sami-Aadis served as Oracles. Later changes like – palm toddy replaced with liquor, the two horns in His crown became three, two ears became four, Salangai (gungurus) took the place of Silambu. These may have occurred as an upgrading part of the decoration process. In olden days, it is said that the Oracle/ Sami-Aadis of Karuppu wore a black dhoti, a helmet-like crown which resembled a buffalo's head, Silambu of brass, finally the knee and wrist silambus, which are extinct now, fortunately these things are used even today by artists of **Theyyam** and **Bhoota-Kola** performers.

Decades ago, the dhoti, silambu, crown etc. were offered to Karuppu as a process of their annual celebrations/ get-togethers by families to whom He served as a tutelary deity, along with swords, sickles, toddy, footwear, meat, clay idols etc.

Oracle wearing Ornaments and Black dress as Karuppu

We must understand that Ayyappa/ Ayyanar/ Saathan are revered gurus who would have a designated sentinel/ guardian, these guardians martyred protecting these gurus of Ajivika. Their weapons like Sangili, Vel, Vaal, Saattai, Urimi etc. would be used as their prefixes like Sangili-Karuppu, Saattai-Adi-Karuppu. Urimi-Maada-Karuppu etc., sometimes prefixes are based on locations. In some accounts, we see Pothuraju, Mhasoba are being replaced by Karuppusamy in the seven-sister cult.

The Southern part of Tamil Nadu, where the sapta-kanyas or sapta-maatas become the fertility goddesses, Karuppusamy usurps the position of Veera Bhadhra and becomes their guardian.

Surprisingly, before the "Bhakti Movement", Karuppu was compared to a demonic force, the king of Goblins, resident of graveyards, wanderer in the deep forests. There is a popular saying –

"

Raavil Katthu Pattaal,
Marathadi Karuppu Adichaal,
Kolli-Vaayan Unnai Azaithaal,
Adangaa-Muni Todarnthaal,
Sami-Aadi Veettin Vazhi

"

Which means, at nights if Katthu (disturbed spirits) possess someone, if a Karuppu hurts/ haunts, if a stubborn Muneeswaran follows you home, run to the exorcist. Annually Karuppu's hunger for blood and meat had to be satisfied. These similarities prove that Pothiraja and Karuppu are the same. Though, Pothiraja, Karuppu and Muniyandi/ Muneeswaran are known as brothers, it is seen that these stories were just to bring them in one frame, yet portraying them different.

Chapter 4:

SUDALAI

This deity also has a puranic birth story. When Parvati wanted a child badly, she is guided by Siva to observe fasting while seated in front of a lamp. While doing so, she tried to adjust the wick of the lamp, during which the lamp scintillates and a spark falls on her lap, out of which MADAN is born (Spark-Tamil-Sudar-Sudalai). Again the suffix MAADAN, to all those associated with the stories of Siva can be commonly seen. The story goes on that, any amount of mother's milk of Parvati did not satiate His hunger. He sneaks out every night to the graveyards and dines on half-burnt and burning corpses. This went on for days, until his bad breadth stirred doubts in the minds of the divine couple. Once they learnt the reason behind this, He was ostracized. He wanders around and reaches the South, where He earns the place of a guardian deity which was granted to Him by a village Goddess. Again, there were many heroes who were given the title 'MAADAN', like Agni-Madan, Sangili-Madan, Sangili-Bhoota-Madan, Mani-Osai-Vel-Madan etc. In these cases too, a Madan who accompanies a Goddess, either stays in her temple or moves with her when she decides to relocate, is none other than Pothiraja.

Sudalaimadan

There are lot of similarities between Sudalai, Pothiraja, Karuppu and 'Pavadairayan' which brings us to a conclusion that all these are the same deity addressed with different names. Firstly, their associations with goblin/ demonic entities, graveyards, animal sacrifices, ruthless behavior and weapons that are commonly found among all these deities. The most important being, the concept of 'Vettai' i.e., hunting, which is similar to the 13th Century witch-hunt in the west. People who dress themselves as these deities run around the village at night, trying to get rid of negative forces and famine. Although Pavadairayan, to whom we can't turn a blind eye, the concept of hunting is no longer practiced.

Tala-Vai-Madan idol with a buffalo head

Here we must observe that 'Thala-Vaai-Madan', a variation in the concept of 'Madan' is the best preserved form of Mhasoba/ Pothuraju, where he is seen with a buffalo head. In recent times, the acceptance of cows and bulls as a sign of purity and supremacy, has overpowered the buffaloes, thus giving him a bull head.

History has witnessed that buffaloes were abundantly found and domesticated, even before the Aryans introduced cows. Thus, Thala-Vaai-Madan is associated with 'Nandi', chief of the 'Bhoota-Ganas' of Siva. Sadly, when devotees are informed about this transition, their feelings are hurt as they have made up their mind that it is a bull's head. His wife 'MADATHI', is compared to 'Durga' just like the case of 'Jogu-Bai' with 'Mhasoba'.

In some versions:

Initially, Tala-Vai-Madan temples had a pillar or a hero-stone like structure that served as the main idol, in the place of worship. Later this deity gained a form as a complete human or a human with cow/ buffalo head. The buffalo head idea is speculative and does not exist now. Whereas, the cow head idea should have sprouted from the idea of associating the deity with Siva or the urge to associate Him with the chief of Siva's goblin army, Nandi. But, in some accounts, he becomes Daksha, Siva's father-in-law. During the annual event in Tala-Vai-Madan's temple, a dead goat is brought back to life, during which a song is sung in His praise where different names are used to describe the deity, in which they call him 'Kaaraane' meaning buffalo in old Tamil texts.

But again, this can be understood only when we try to omit the puranic backstories. These pre-vedic deities who happen to exist, even before the Vedas were introduced (made its way-in), these deities were too simple and were bound to no rules. As we know that puranas were composed only around 6th to 10th Century, the dates are still speculative, but, we still can witness that new details are included, creating new editions till date. This will still continue in the future. The augmentation of puranas is seen to be perpetual.

Having learnt about the different categories of Karuppu, the topic of Karuppu is so intense and deep that we could not study and understand its concept wholly.
He is being treated as a Tantric God, just like in the case of Betal, Bootharadhana, Theyyam, Mahisandayya etc. and is just too complex to comprehend. All that can be concluded is that – Karuppu has various names (prefixes and suffixes), stories, practices, versions etc.

He has a huge 'Fan Base' in Southern Tamil Nadu, giving rise to independent Karuppu temples, where He does not have to guard any other deities. Instead, it's seen that He stands alone at the frontiers of a village, guarding His people.

As a Kshetrapal, Karuppu is often associated with Bhairav, Veera Bhadhra, and Sri Krishna etc. This confusion is due to the way He is portrayed in His idol form, Holding sword, aruvaal (sickle), a dog besides Him etc. Initially, when He has no forms, just a veergal or nadukkal, He remains untouched by the Puranas. When Karuppu becomes the protector of the frontiers, His names take more puranic shades like 'Uggira-Bhathran', 'Agora-Veera-Bhathran', 'Uggira-Bhairavan', 'Uggira-Karuppu' etc. He is later given 'Parivara-Devathas' to accompany Him. Resulting in more variations in His stories to glorify Him.

Chapter 5:

PAVADAIRAYAN

The story of Pavadairayan, keeps us wondering about how the name itself is giving Pothuraju a new identity, His story is as goes –

He is born to 'Periyandavar' and 'Periyandachi' (no specific names mentioned anywhere, hence these names should have been a title to address a chief or a captain of a tribe), who are the chiefs of a 'decoit' clan, the region where they existed is still speculated. This childless couple pray to Siva, who at that time was wandering and begging. It so happened that the arrogant Brahma's fifth head was slayed by Siva and Brahma's skull stuck to Siva's hand and was cursed to feed himself through alms. He reaches the place where Periyandachi assumes Siva to be a 'Shaivaite Sage' – 'Siva-Thondar', asks him to bless her. He offers her a pinch of Vibuthi (Sacred ash), saying a son would be born to her, who is an avatar of Siva. In some versions, a son, who would be a great king in the future, the puranic versions of His story are multiple, hence can't rely to exact one kind. A few years later, a son is born to Periyandavar and Periyandachi, and they name Him 'KALVIKATHAAN'. They made sure He is trained in all the war-crafts and weaponries. The story says He was indifferent to His family's occupation, as He felt it was reprehensive.

He walks into a dense forest, where He hears the laughter of a woman. Scared Kalvikathaan assumes it to be a 'Kollivai' or 'Vana-Pisachi'. Later a voice says, "Fear Not! It is me, the primordial Goddess of the Universe". He then discovers a sculpture of 'AGNALAMMA' in the forest, for whom He builds a temple. The Goddess was once curious to test His devotion and asks Him to offer her His organs. 'Kalvikathaan' immediately cuts open His torso and places all his insides (organs) on the skirt of the Goddess, impressed by which she calls Him 'Pavadairayan'. Though the original version says, Devi Angalamma was offered meat, alcohol, 'padayal' (feast in Tamizh) and hungry 'Kalvikathaan' fed from the left overs that was scattered on the Goddess's skirt, while she ate. Looking at His innocence, she called Him, 'Pavadarairayan' – meaning 'King of Skirts'.

Pavadairayan's most common form in Tamil Nadu

Finally, every version of His story ends with a boon granted to Him by Devi Angalamma, to be the guardian deity of her temple, granting Him a demi-god status.

Here we must understand that the concept of Devi Angalamma transits from Andhra Pradesh up to the Northern parts of Tamil Nadu, later ended up in few places of Karnataka. In Andhra, she is 'ANKAMMA'/ 'ANKALAMMA', when she touches the borders of Tamil Nadu, due to the Tamizh dialect, she becomes 'ANGALAMMA'. When the puranas take-over/ absorb Angalamma, she becomes 'ANGALA PARAMESHWARI'. Though there are numerous Angalamma temples erected newly in Tamil Nadu and Karnataka now, to reach the origin, we need to trace the travel route of the concept, of Ankamma or Angalamma. Where we understand that **POTHURAJU,** who is seated beside her or in front of her or at the entrance, takes a new name 'PADAVAIRAYAN' with a new puranic story. Hence, Pothuraju with His new name Pavadairayan has temples only in the Northern parts of Tamil Nadu. Even today we see that all the Ankamma temples of Telangana and Andhra have Pothuraju as her guardian.

We can see how in Tamil Nadu alone, this deity has various forms, names, roles, stories etc., due to the cultural exchanges and puranic influences. In Kerala, Pothiraja/ Karuppu is seen as a part of 'SASTHA' (AYYAPPAN) pantheon, but vaguely to any goddesses. The only thing that connects is the buffalo He is associated with.

KERALA –

In Kerala we can witness both the forms i.e., 'SAATHAN' and 'MAADAN'. Saathan, a word from the '**Vanigam/ Vanigar**' community, addressing their God (a possible ancestor), makes its way into Kerala. The carriers being 'Cheras' and 'Pandyas'. 'Maadan', is a derivative of 'Sudalai Madan' of the Tamizh region. There are stories in Kerala where a goddess, accompanied by a Maadan, who protects her while searching for a new place to settle, just like Pothiraja. Here 'Sathan' from the Vanigar community becomes 'SASTHAN' due to the dialect.

Chapter 6:

VISHNUMAYA CHATHAN

Residing in 'Perungottakara' near Trisur – KL, is the 'Vishnumaya Chathan' temple. 'CHATHAN' should have been a corrupt pronunciation of 'SATHAN'. The Arabs who stayed at the Malabar region, were the reason of cultural exchange and conversions. When 'Mappilla' community grew in number, their new religious beliefs spread in Kerala, similarly the deities of Kerala became the ghosts of the Arab nations. As idol worship is strictly prohibited in Islam, the local tantric deity of Kerala i.e., 'SATHAN' had to face calumny in the west. He was called 'SHATHAN', later 'SHAITHAN' by the Muslims, finally 'SATAN' in the Biblical texts.

Vishnumaya Chathan in Kerala

6.1 STORIES IN THE LAND OF MALAYALAM

6.1.1 The story of SATHAN, according to the priests of Vishnumaya Temple –

Once Siva visits a forest in Kerala, to hunt. Wandering alone in the forest, he hears a voice so melodious and mesmerizing. It was none other than 'KOOLIVAAKA', the daughter of the 'Chandala' chief of 'KOOLIVANA'. He instantly is attracted to her, like under a spell. Further it is seen that, he asks her to stay there until he returned from his hunt. Scared of Siva's wrath, also being a devotee of Parvati, Koolivaaka is confused. She didn't want to be the reason of Parvati's anger, by having sex with the goddess's husband. She falls on her knees and prays to Parvati, who instantly appears. Parvati is seen smiling, explaining to Koolivaaka that this incident was pre-ordained by Parvati herself.

In her previous birth, Koolivaaka was a maid of Parvati in 'Kailasa', by the name 'Manaswani'. When Ganesha was hungry, he couldn't be consoled and constantly cried. To stop him, not waiting for Parvati to respond to the situation, she breastfeeds Ganesha. The sight of a maid feeding her child enraged Parvati, ended up cursing her to be born as a Chandala woman. She further explains that this birth of Koolivaaka was for a divine cause, to raise the child of Siva and Parvati. Explaining this, Parvati took the form of Koolivaaka waiting to unite with Siva. A child is born of their union, and a buffalo is left there to guard the child, by Siva. (In some versions, the child is hurt in the forest, with pain unbearable, he rests on a buffalo. Later, the buffalo follows him everywhere.). Later Koolivaaka is informed about the child, who was abandoned in the forest. She raises the child as her own and breastfeeds him. He is raised by the tribe for seven (7) years. On his seventh birthday, 'Narada' visits him to inform him about his birth. The kid is advised by Narada and the other retinue of the tribe to visit his parents in Kailasa. The 7-year-old boy, mounts his buffalo, playing ‘Ezhara’ (musical instrument) heads to Kailasa. ‘Nandi’, the guardian deity of Kailasa blocks him from meeting Siva. The boy who had the power of taking myriad forms, took the form of Vishnu, enters Kailasa and meets Siva and Parvati. The couple are happy to meet their son, blesses the boy with various magical powers and called him ‘Maya’, because he took the form of Vishnu, he was called ‘Vishnumaya’.

Parvati then informs the boy that he was born to defeat the demon ‘Jalandhara’ and bids him farewell. Vishnumaya finds the place where Jalandhara lived and challenges him for a duel, which went on for months. Finally he takes the form of ‘Chakra’ and chases Jalandhara, leaving no place to hide, Jalandhara’s head is slayed by the Chakra.

The story continues, that, after his victory over Jalandhara, he re-unites with his tribe, where he learns that a demon named ‘Briga’ has been abusing his mother Koolivaaka, to marry him. Vishnumaya, mounts his buffalo again, goes in search of Briga. He is accompanied by none, as everyone were scared of Briga’s ten most powerful weapons that could kill even the gods. Vishnumaya was hurt during a fierce battle with Briga, where his blood drops gave birth to 400 goblins.

It is later said that his assistant ‘Karikutty/ Karimkutty’, assists him during the war where the ten weapons of Briga were swallowed by the ten goblins, killing the goblins instantly. Vishnumaya takes the form of a Chakra and slays Briga. Hence, making Him the king of 390 powerful goblins or ‘KUTTY-CHATHANS’, It is said that in ‘Treta-Yuga’, he was born as bow-and-arrow of Rama, in ‘Dwapara-Yuga’, chakra of Sri Krishna, finally in ‘Kali-Yuga’ as ‘Vishnumaya Chathan’. He is seen riding a buffalo, holding Ezhara, a musical instrument, ‘Kapala’ (bowl), ‘Kuruvedi’ (stick/ staff).

Though the story is too contradicting in many places, as for instance –

- Initially the maid is cursed for breastfeeding Parvati's child, later it is seen that she ends up doing the same for Vishnumaya, the son of the divine couple.

- The dhanusu (bow) of Rama/ Vishnu - 'Sharnga', Mace – 'Koumudaki', Counch – 'Panchajanya' and Sword – 'Nandaka' are weapons who are born as human beings according to puranas, even weapons were treated as life-forms by the Aryans.

- Vishnumaya as 'Sudarsana Chakra' is again too contradictory, as 'Karthaveeryanjuna' is already mentioned as 'Chakra-Avatari' (an incarnation of Sudarsana in the puranas).

- Travelling on a buffalo, ascending mouth Kailasa, is another point that lacks logic and sounds too magical.

- Jalandhara rakshasa, existed even before Rama and Krishna were born. He is the husband of 'Vrinda/ Tulasi' and the puranas mention his death to have occurred in the hands of Siva.

Overall, Vishnumaya or Chathan is a tribal pre-vedic deity of Kerala, associated with an Indian water buffalo, who demands offerings and sacrifices similar to Karuppusamy or Pothuraju.

6.1.2 In THEYYAM culture –

In the classic Kerala tradition of Theyyam worship, almost all the deities have a Theyyam form. 'Theyyam', from 'Dheyyam', again from the word 'DHEIVAM' which means divine. Theyyams are of various kinds, some of them are gods (puranic) and the rest are heroes who built this society. Keeping aside the puranic influence on the stories of each of these characters (Theyyams), we see that some of the deities are pre-vedic and were later absorbed into puranas or given a puranic status as an upgrade. 'Vishnu Maya' too was a pre-vedic tantric deity/ a totem worship, he was the king of goblins and evil spirits, just like in the case of 'KARUPPU', 'POTHURAJU', 'SUDALAI MADAN' etc. He is pleased through tantric methods, sacrifices and more. He holds a special place in Theyyam rituals of Kerala by the name 'KUTTY CHATHAN THEYYAM'. He is often understood as a young, mischievous, naughty, evil, creates illusions and also who protects His devotees. The play or the performance of Kutty Chathan Theyyam is performed by wearing a buffalo mask. We can also see that there are few more Theyyam characters that are associated with buffaloes like 'Guligan', 'Pottan', and 'Pothy-Theyyam' etc. All these Theyyams are the branches of the same tree 'Vishnumaya'.

»

Finally, Vishnumaya, when studied without a puranic background story, has been the deity of the ignoble and weak. What was Vishnumaya called before he was associated with Siva, Parvati, Vishnu or puranas, no one knows. But there is no story of Vishnumaya with precise and detailed mentions in any puranas. The temple itself is 400-years-old and it has been given the color of 'Agama-Neeti', which totally diverts its purpose of 'access-to-all'. Vishnumaya, He who can fulfill any of his devotees' wishes, also punishes with no remorse. In olden days when travelers from Tamil Nadu who went to Kerala walking through dense forests looking for a living, claimed to have witnessed

‘Vishnumaya’ in the deep forests, which are now the reserve forests, at the Kerala-Tamil Nadu border. They called Him ‘MALAYALA KARUPPU’ (not to be confused with ‘PADINETTAM-PADI-MALAYALA-KARUPPU in Alagar temple). He is said to be naughty, creates an illusion, so surreal that any person can lose his mind, never returns home and is finally consumed by the 390-goblins of Vishnumaya. He is a trickster, very strict, also is playful. There are accounts of witnesses claiming to have seen Him on a buffalo in dense forests, not pardoning who enters His territory with bad intentions, very similar to the behavior of ‘MULA-MAYSONDAYYA’ (the buffalo headed Kola of Karnataka).

Guligan-theyyam, with a weird mask (sometimes compared to a buffalo’s mask or face) is said to be a form of Siva sometimes associated with ‘Yama’. Guligan-theyyam is also called ‘Gulika’ in the Bhootakola tradition of ‘Karavali’, South Canara of Karnataka. He is a goblin, protector of lower castes and tribes. Similarly Pottan-theyyam is another form of Siva, a Chandala, who had an argument with ‘Aadi Sankaracharya’ (this story should have been a later development about this deity). Sadly, Pothy/ Pothu Theyyam does not exist anymore or maybe it does exist in a different name, form or a story that associates Him with some other deity. But, Pothu-theyyam is still practiced in the Karavali regions, ‘Kodagu’ and Karnataka as ‘MAYSANDAYYA-KOLA’, where Kola is the name given to Theyyam performances in ‘Tulu’ region. MAYSANDAYYA or ‘MAYSONDAY’, initially was ‘MAHIS-ANNAYYA’ (just like the ‘Varaha’ is called ‘PANJURLI-ANNAPPA’). ‘Appa’ and ‘Ayya’ are the terms that denote respect. The corruption occurred due to the local dialect Mahis-annayya, Maysaandayya, later becomes Maysonday.

Note: Just like the mispronunciation of ‘Muneeswara’ (a warrior sage) as ‘MUNIYANDI’, he who is known as ‘MAILARA-LINGA’ in Karnataka, ‘MALLANNA’ in Andhra Pradesh, ‘KHANDOBA’ in Maharastra. A typical example of how languages create an impact so strong that can create different identities for the same persona.

Chapter 7:

MULA MAYSONDAYYA

In the 'Karavali' region of Karnataka, 'Tulunad', 'South Canara', 'Kodagu' and northern most parts of Kerala, Bhoota-kola art is widely practiced. Bhoota-kola is a celebration of the spirits of the deceased and powerful divine spirits. Here Mula-Maysondayya plays a very important role, he is considered one of the most powerful bhootas. Nowadays, in some places. 'NANDIKONA-BHOOTA', which is a form of 'Nandi' or the bull-spirit is often confused with Maysonday-bhoota for various reasons, which lack logic. Although there are many common deities among the Bhoota and Theyyam performances, most of them are now confused, losing their originality and what they stand for. Guligan in Theyyam, is a kids-loving playful Theyyam, while in Kola, Gulika becomes unmerciful, unforgivable, wrathful guardian deity of 'Panjurli' (Varaha), who chewed on a finger of Vishnu. Similarly, Vishnumaya-Kutti-Chathan and Mula-Maysonday are sometimes portrayed different in these art forms, but both should have been originated from Totemic worship.

Totemic worship - an animal that has a spiritual significance, is later adopted as an emblem or symbol by a set of tribal clans and for tantric practices.

7.1 STORIES IN THE LAND OF KARUNADU

'Mula Maisondaya' – in the land of Tulunad, the deities like Sapta Kanyas do not have much importance, instead they are replaced with 'Siri' worship or the 'Sapta Siri' Pooja. Siri worship is a women oriented cult, meant for women and worshipped by them. But, there is a twist, like in the concept of Sapta Kanyas, where they are guarded by Pothuraju (Veera Bhadhra, puranic influence), seven (7) Siris do not have a male guardian deity. A 'Siri kumara' sits beside them, whom the 7 Siris guard, the son of Siris.

Maisonday – Bhootakola performer with Buffalo mask

Another interesting fact/ transition occurs here, Mhasoba/ Pothuraju who is Mahisasura himself, becomes an independent deity as Maisondaya Bhoota totally disassociated from the 7 Siris. The native story of the land that explains the struggle of 7 women/ 7 stages of a woman, who attains divinity just like the case of 'ANDRU PIRANTHU', 'ANDRE MARAINDHA MUTHALAMMAN' and her 6 sisters in Tamil Nadu – not to be confused with other MUTHALAMMAN temples of Tamil Nadu. The stories associated with these 7 women is always tragic, stressful, involves domestic violence and finally attaining divinity through course of fate. That is another reason why it's a women cult, here women vent out their stress (relating themselves with the deities) during the worship or rituals of these 7 sisters.

7.1.1 The story of SIRI:

The longest 'PADDAM' or 'POETRY' of Tulu is 'Siri Paddanna'. The story of a 'Bunt' princess, the 7 Siris or 'ELVERU Sirikulu'. A short summary of this story of how the princess Siri and the 6 other Siris, representing the hardships and struggles, a woman undergoes / experiences in her life. These struggles bring these women together to form a cult of Siri {7 Siris: the primary Siri 'Akkeresa Siri', 'Sonne', 'Ghinde', 'Daru', 'Abbaga', 'Darage' and 'Siri Kumara'}.

Story: According to the Tulunadu custom, it is the son-in-law who inherits or the offspring of the son-in-law inherits the properties. This custom is called 'ALIYA-KATTU' or 'ALIYA-SANTANA', which is observed in parts of Kerala too.

'SOMALA DEVI', a princess of 'Satyanapura', is married to 'Bermalwa'. They were childless, so they begged 'Bermer' of 'Satyanapura (an ancestor of his wife's lineage), to grant them a child. Bermer (Bermer's spirit) in the disguise of a Brahmin visited their house, but vanished in thin air leaving a stone box. From inside the stone box they heard a child cry. 'Bermalwa' named her Siri (Akkeresa Siri).

She was married to a man of royal bloodline, who posed himself as a man of morals. Siri gets pregnant, her happy husband decides to gift her a saree. While on the way back home, he meets his mistress (prostitute) who tries the saree on her though he forbids her from doing so. He gifts the saree to Siri on her baby shower. Siri, who is born with divine powers, immediately realizes that it was used by a prostitute earlier, insults her husband in front of the guests. Her furious husband decides to teach her a lesson.

A child is born and Siri's father dies as per the astrologer's prediction. The newborn's sight had killed the grandfather. Later a distant relative of Siri's father tries to covet the property which was rightfully Siri's, shockingly Siri's husband testifies against her. Her curse burns down the palace, she announces a divorce to her husband and walks away with her child 'Kumara' and maid 'Daru' (second Siri).

She walked where paths led her, she goes through a lot of troubles and sufferings by the men she encounters on her way. Finally, two brothers (princes) adopt her, as their sister and requests her to stay with them, upon listening to her story. But her son Kumara refuses to stay saying he does not want to be raised in someone else's house. He felt a lack of belonging. She blesses him to become a (Daiva) demi-god. Later it's seen that Daru too refuses to stay with her as she felt her sole purpose was to take care of Kumara. Daru was also blessed by Siri to become a Daiva.

The two brothers arranges a remarriage for Siri, this marriage turns out to be blissful. But, she learns that her new husband was already married to a woman called 'SAMU' (third Siri). Samu and Siri initially had lot of misunderstandings, later they make amends. Siri gives birth to a girl, 'SONNE' (fourth Siri). Siri hands over the child to Samu and instructs her to leave the child at the doorstep of 'Chandu'. She further grants her divinity and blesses her to become a Daiva once she accomplishes the task. Samu leaves the baby at the doorstep, slips from the threshold, hurts her temple and dies.

Sonne is raised by Chandu, but Chandu is worried that Sonne did not bleed though she reached her teens. He finds an abandoned Brahmin girl 'GINDE' (fifth Siri), brings her home and raises her as his own. Later he prays to Bermer for the sake of Sonne as she had to be married to someone and still did not bleed due to the hormonal imbalance. He promises to build a temple for Bermer. Sonne soon matures. Sonne is married to 'Gurumarla'. This childless couple pray to Bermer again, makes promises of offerings and sacrifices. Immediately they are blessed with twins – 'ABBAGA' and 'DARAGE' (sixth and seventh Siris).

Bermer, in the guise of a Brahmin, tries to remind the couple about their promises. They insult and shoo him away. He reaches the house of Sonne, when Sonne and her husband are out searching for suitable grooms. The twins were playing ‘Chenne Mane’. Due to a petty fight in the game, one hits the other with a wooden game board and the girl dies. The surviving twin scared of murder, throws the dead twin into a well and accidentally slips into the well as well and drowns. Bermer appears to Sonne and her husband and derided them that this was the result of their misdeeds.

Here we see these seven women have no protector/ guardian/ companion. Maisonday or Pothuraju becomes an independent deity.

7.1.2 MAISONDAY:

He is associated with Mysuru and coastal regions of Karnataka’s Bhoota worship. The newly sprouted/ self-made Hindu groups have no clue about the culture of South India. Mahisa/ Mhasoba is worshipped since centuries in different parts of South India. The documentation of historians are still available. These self-proclaiming protectors of Hinduism powered by Aryan influences even today, are trying to eradicate this deity.

‘Aliyakattu’ and ‘Bhootaaradhane’ are deeply rooted into the worship of many spirits that include ‘Mahisasura’. Aliyakattu – son in law, the legal heir is practiced by the non-brahmin communities. The idea of this is adapted in puranas by Brahmins. Example, the daughters carry their father’s name and not the sons, like 1) Dakshayini, the daughter of Daksha, 2) Drupad – Draupadi, 3) Janak – Janaki, 4) Parvataraj – Parvati etc.
This very idea shows that these characters or concepts prevailed before the Brahmin community influenced the country.

There are various names and stories of Mahisasura (associating the term 'Asura' to evil should have been an Aryan ideology). 'Kundodara, 'Pothulayya', 'Pothuraju', 'Mahisandayya' etc. They all are the names of a ruler, who once ruled Mysuru (Mahisa-Ooru). Aliya-Kattu has its origins from Mahisasura himself, there are various books published regarding the same. In Tulunadu, Mahisa's benevolence earned him the name 'Bhootapandya'. Here the historians have mentioned that Chanda-Munda who were slayed by Chamundi were actually not rakshasas. But, they were the tribes that were native/ inhabitants of Karnataka – the Chandala and Munda tribe, who were subdued during Aryan invasion, and to mark their defeat, the queen (Chamundi) was given the name 'Chanda'Munda-Vinashini'.

Udipi Krishna's mutt, absorbed the Bhoota-Daiva Mahisasura, by the name 'Bhootaraja'. Dr. Ma. Sa. Achyut Sarma in his book: "UDIPI KSHETRADA NAIJA CHITRA MATTHHU CHARITIKA HINNELE", has mentioned clearly how Udipi mutt, worships Mahisasura.

The Hindu groups, who call themselves the saviors of Hinduism, promote the worship of cows. But we, in the south, simply do not have mentions of the practice or rituals of worshipping cows in any of our old literatures. Instead we have a few mentions of buffaloes and how were they an integral part of the lives of our ancestors, In Sangam text, we see that a bride-to-be, places her ornaments and wedding saree in between the horns of a buffalo before adorning herself on the wedding day. This shows that buffaloes were considered auspicious. Also the rope that went through the nostrils of a buffalo, was burnt, mixed with castor oil, to prepare kohl, which people believed, to have the ability to ward off evil. Similarly, buffalo worship is part of Tulunad's Bhootaaradhane.

Chapter 8:

BHOOTHARAJA

A classic example of how various influences create various identities for the same persona. This deity has been influenced by various sects for every 100 KMS in the state of Karnataka giving rise to different genres of him. Starting from the pre-vedic period to the 'Dwaita Philosophy' of the Madhavas, has given birth to different flavors of Bhootharaja.

Bhootharaja Swamy's common form

8.1 Pre-Vedic:

The Somakunita is another form of folk art like the Bhootha-Kola and Theyyam performances. This too is an art form of Karnataka, also called 'Bhoothakunita', which are deeply rooted into 'the concept of Bhootharaja'. Soma/ Bhootakunita still struggles to find a space to breathe for its survival. Men who perform this art wear huge wooden masks, silver and brass ornaments to adore themselves. Their attire is eye-catchy, walks ahead of the procession, during festive seasons of temples. There are different colored masks differentiating them, to whom these Bhootharayas serve, example: 1) Kencha Bhootharaya – red mask – guardian of Vishnu; 2) Mangala Bhootharaya – yellow mask – serves Siva; 3) Kariya Bhootharaja – black mask/ sometimes blue – Bhairav himself etc. Their performances are supported by folk instruments like 'Tumte', 'Dollu', 'Mouri', 'Sadde' etc. They carry a snake shaped staff called 'Nagabetha'. Also we see the similarities of Pothuraju, Karuppu and Betal in these deities, as they carry a whip to ward-off evil, they lash the devotees and themselves, and we can see kids are being handed to them, to bless the kids with courage.

There are various stories of how a 'Siva-Gana' or a demon or in some cases Kal Bhairav himself is appointed to guard the goddess. Also, there is a popular folklore about how a newly married girl, bids farewell from her maternal home, accompanied by her father-in-law who came to escort her to her husband. On that unfortunate evening, she had a sudden urge to urinate. She requests her father-in-law to face away from the place where she was urinating.

For a fraction of a second, lust sprouted in his mind, and his inappropriate stare enraged the daughter-in-law. She entered a snake's anthill/ mound and came out as a goddess with two bhootas or demons beside her and killed the father-in-law. Later she becomes a village goddess with a Bhootharaja alongside her protecting her at all times.

There is another story very similar - 'Pacchaiamman' in Tamil Nadu. The supreme goddess who decides to perform penance/ tapas, settles in a forest. Feeling pity of her situation Vishnu, Siva, Bhairav etc. descended in the form of 'Semmuni (red)' – Kencha Bhootha, Kariappa – 'Karumuni (black)', Mangala – 'Agnimuni (yellow), blue – 'Jadamuni' etc. Though the idea is common among the Tamils and Kannadigas, the rituals stand distinct from each other. In Tamil Nadu they are offered meat and toddy, whereas for the performers of Somakunita: Banana, Honey, Coconut, powdered cardamom mixture is offered, only the goddess becomes the recipient of toddy and meat.

8.2 The Migrated Bhootharaja:

The Bhootharaja, Bhootharaya, Bhoothappa etc. are all different names of Bhootharaja or Pothuraju himself. There are several examples like 'Hanagere', 'Chikmagaluru', 'Mudigere', 'Nidasangi' etc. where He is an independent deity and in several other accounts He becomes a guardian, brother or a companion of goddesses like Chowdeshwari, Padmavati, Maramma etc. We can see that Pothuraju in Andhra and Telangana, is with Chowdeshwari and different forms of Yellamma, very similar to Bhootharaja guarding the village goddesses of Karnataka. The idea, characteristics, offerings, placement of the deity, associated weapons and the day of worship (new moon day) does not differ a bit, just like in the case of Pothuraju, Karuppu, Sudalai and Betal.

Here Bhootharaja, in Karnataka initially had a hero stone-like structure for worship, surrounded by weapons like Trident/ Trishul and swords. Trident, might have been a recent development, after the association of Bhootharaja with Siva. In some temples like 'Hanagere', He does not have a specific form, instead He is believed to be seated on a tree along with His younger sister Chowdeshwari. One might be startled at the sight of thousands of locks in and around the temple, this ritual of fastening a lock in a temple's vicinity can be seen in a few Karuppusamy temples as well.

This concept of Bhootharaja has a mirrored image in Southern parts of Tamil Nadu, by the name 'Bhoothathar'. This deity is given a prefix – 'Sangili' which means chained, in some areas. This deity is adorned with iron chains, fastening Him, to have a control on his wrath. In some accounts, the devotees offer chains along with the regular offerings, and sacrifices are made like in case of any other pre-vedic deities. Sangili Bhoothathar's origin or the story without the influence of Puranas is still unavailable. Bhoothathar is usually believed to reside on trees with few other demi-gods and ghastly spirits. Bhoothathar in some places guard 'Ayyanar', this may have occurred due to the mix-and-match of cultures with the neighboring locations. Hence, there is a widespread confusion between Karuppu and Bhoothathar. Although both the deities are same, the devotees do not feel comfortable with this idea.

Bhoothathar, who is also called 'Mundan' in some places, is seen with a consort called 'Isakki' (in some versions – 'Bramha Shakti'). Ironically, in some locations, Isakki becomes the wife of another local male deity, although the story of Isakki describes her as an independent deity. Isakki, a derivative of the word 'Yakshi', who was once a married woman. The 'Villupaattu' artists narrate that she was murdered/ committed suicide, later her spirit appealed to the almighty for a second chance, not for herself, but for the sake of her kids, who were abandoned after her demise. She is then blessed to become a 'Yakshini' and it is said that she took care of her kids and their lineage as a guardian deity.

8.3 Absorption into the Madhava Mutt:

The Madhava Mutt's narration states that Narayana Sharma, who was a disciple of Vaadiraja. Narayana Sharma, in his previous consecutive births, committed a lot of sins and misdeeds. Sri Vaadiraja took him as a disciple. Once another Madhava Mutt guru visited Vaadiraja, he was Vyasaraya, a staunch Vaishnavite. His regular 'Dwadashi

Pooja' had to be performed, but in Vaadiraja's mutt. He did not want to perform the Pooja without Vaadiraja participating with him. Later it is seen that both the gurus Vyasaraya and Vaadiraja had lunch together and for some reason Vaadiraja advised his disciples to stay back in the mutt and not follow him. Using his yoga-sakthi, Vaadiraja brought back all the food he had consumed, from his stomach, and laid them on a plantain leaf, just the way it was served. The curious Narayana Sharma witnessed this miracle, hiding behind a tree. The guru Vaadiraja noticed his disciple Narayana Sharma defying his orders, cursed him to become a brahma-rakshasa/ demon.

Later it is seen that Vaadiraja himself encounters this demon and releases him from his curse. He also commands him to serve as his guard and fulfill the desires of his devotees who visits his mutt. A 'Bali' ritual is conducted for Bhootharaja (Vishnu Sharma) in the mutt, by offering coconuts, vermillion, in some cases pumpkins.

Although these stories, narrated by the Madhava Brahmins may have been a process of including a pre-vedic deity into their mutt culture, or during the process of establishing their mutt in a location, of an already existing deity of that location.

8.4 Bhootharaja of the Villages:

Here we see a mix of all the flavors of Bhootharaja genres. He becomes Siva, Bhairav, Veer Bhadhra, Siva-gana of Kailasa, Demon, even traces of Mhasoba tradition. This is a perfect example of how the people from rural areas accept and relate their deity to 'anything divine', with no mental barriers. Thus, letting the deity free and unbound, making it accessible emotionally. Here too, Bhootharaja, like in the case of Karuppu, stands independent, and very few cases with a goddess. Although the concept of 'Paari-Vettai' (patrolling the village at night on a horse) is missing, the rest remains the same.

In Tamil Nadu, there are temples of Kali and many other furious goddesses, who are accompanied by a guardian (idol) that resembles Bhoothathar or Betal, who is none other than Bhootharaja himself. Few decades ago, these guardian deities of the goddesses who were present inside the temple vicinity, were portrayed as evil magicians and asuras/ rakshasas, with new improbable stories of being punished by the goddesses. Hence, the devotees slap/ spank/ step-on/ sometimes cuss these idols before entering the sanctum. Well, "ignorance is not always a bliss".

Chapter 9:

URAMMA & MARIKAMBE – BUFFALO/ EMME/ KONA

9.1 URAMMA:

She is a village deity, to whom devotees sacrifice a buffalo annually. She is a tutelary deity to many lower caste communities. It is said that she was married to a buffalo king earlier, whom she later kills. Hence a buffalo is married to the goddess every year, sacrificing the previous one. The blood is collected in a brass utensil as a part of ritual and the head is placed at the deity's feet just like the case of 'BULKAMPET YELLAMMA TEMPLE' (which is now banned). Although these practices have been brought to an end, there are villages even now practicing this ritual. The village goddesses are often associated with water buffalo sacrifices due to their marriage with a male deity 'Buffalo King'. Initially, a buffalo is carefully selected and dedicated to the goddess called 'Devara-Pothu' or 'Gauda-Kona', husband of the divine. In some places she does not turn widow even for a day, by marrying another buffalo, a day before decapitating the previous buffalo on the annual ceremony. Similar case being, Goddess 'Yellamma' of Savadatti/ Saundatti turns widow for a day and becomes a married woman again. But, the Brahmins replaced the practice of buffalo marriage by marrying Yellamma to a Brahmin sage called 'Jamadagni'.

Like Andhra and Telangana where Pothuraju is represented by a twin structure of either wood or stone, where the goddess sits in between or beside. In villages of Karnataka, a few decades ago, the buffalo king was represented by a wooden post, sometimes a stone pillar that symbolizes a 'Phallus'. The wooden post was decorated with flowers, turmeric and oil lamps, in front of which the buffaloes were sacrificed. After the ritual, once the buffaloes (husband of the goddess) were decapitated, the wooden post was uprooted, the goddess was turned widow by divesting her ornaments. This wooden post was burnt later. This idea of wooden post/ stone pillar was later adopted by the 'Agamashastra' of temple construction by calling it the 'Dwaja-Sthamb'.

To represent the animals that the gods or goddesses are associated with, the Dwaja-Sthamb/ flag-post bears an image/ idol of that animal. Not necessarily these animals were to be sacrificed, in some cases, these animals were symbols or totems associated with the deity or cult.

This ritual of planting a wooden post called 'PANTHA- KAAL NADUVAL' is observed in Tamil Nadu, Andhra Pradesh and parts of Karnataka, where a wooden post is planted before marriage, annual ceremony in temples etc. A goat or a rooster is selected and decapitated/ sacrificed to the post hoping to block any obstructions during the planned event. This wooden post is none other than Pothuraju/ Mhasoba/ Maisandaya himself.

9.2 MARIKAMBE/ MARIAMMA:

In this story we see that, how a goddess (village/ tribal deity) is absorbed into the Aryan puranas. The goddess like 'NRITTI', 'KALI', 'MAARI', 'URAMMA' etc. become the wives of Siva and they turn against the non-brahmin crowd in some cases. This demeaning act was done to establish the superiority of the Aryan Brahmins over the natives. Such changes are still witnessed in temples and poojas where a Janehu/ Janjyam/ Poonool is put on to the idols by the Brahmin priests to claim their rights over the deities. In some cases, they create stories about these 'native deities', to be born in Brahmin communities.

Story: MARIKE is a Brahmin girl, who falls head over heels for a very handsome man, not knowing the fact that he is a 'Chandala'. They are happy and cling to each other at all times. They give birth to seven children. One day Marike's mother-in-law pays visit to her son, Marike prepares sweets for her (Sihi-Kadubu). She leaves the house, hides behind the hut trying to eavesdrop. All she wanted to know was her mother-in-law's opinion about her. But she is shocked to hear the mother-in-law say, "No sweets can match the taste and texture of buffalo MEAT". She is furious when she learns that her husband hid the fact, that he was a Chandala. She kills her husband while the mother-in-law flees the scene. She also decides to kill all her kids but, the seventh child flees in fright. She curses her own son that 'he' and all his descendants will be considered low-born. It is said that in the next life, after immolating herself, she is born as 'Marikambe' and her husband 'a buffalo'. Thus, sacrificing a buffalo will satiate her anger. Now in places like 'Sirsi Marikambe Temple', a buffalo is dedicated to 'Maari' but not sacrificed.

Marikambe is one out of the seven 'Sapta Kanyas', in the frontiers of a village. In some stories like 'Sapta Siri', 'ANDRU PIRANTHU', 'ANDRE MARAINDHA MUTHALAMMAN' in Tamil Nadu, we see that these seven-women cult have not been influenced much, instead it remains unaltered or true to its original. But in most regions, this seven-women cult is now under the brahminical influence by the names 'Brahmi', 'Maheshwari', 'Koumari', 'Vaishnavi', 'Varahi', 'Indrani' and 'Chamunda'. These deities, who were formless, under open-sky, layman's gods, were recipients of meat, are now subjected to rituals and newly composed 'Mantras' and 'Hymns'.

9.3 RENUKA as 'Yellamma'/ 'Gangamma':

The puranic story describes her marital struggle with sage Jamadagni. She mothers four children, sometimes three, in some versions fourteen. She is described as the sexual energy of the Universe, where she demands her husband for sexual satisfaction, who fails her as he grew older. She is then punished for desiring a Yaksha (sometimes Gandharva), by her husband. Jamadagni then commands his son to decapitate Renuka. Her head is worshipped as 'Mari', 'Yellamma', 'Gangamma' etc. She is the goddess of rain, fertility and guardian of the frontiers where she blocks evil spirits, famine and plague from entering a village, just like 'Pidari' and 'Ilakkumi'.

Goddess married to wooden staff – Pothuraju

The pattern of these pre-vedic rituals, during the annual ceremony for Gangamma/ Pochamma/ Yellamma in Andhra Pradesh and borders of Karnataka, were totally different. A wooden or stone staff is placed beside the idol of the goddess. During the annual ceremony, which lasts for eleven to fourteen days, a buffalo is sacrificed on a final day, where the heads of a buffalo, a goat and a rooster are carried on the head of the priest, who circumambulates the sanctum of the goddess (it is believed that it would rain that very night). The ceremony ends with the goddess getting married to the stone/ wooden staff, who is Pothuraju/ Pothiraja.

Fertility goddess married to the stone staff (Pothuraju)

Although we may now see that these wooden staffs have been replaced with Siva-Linga in most of the temples, making Yellamma/ Gangamma the wife of Siva. In Draupadi temples (Andhra Pradesh, Tamil Nadu and parts of Karnataka), we see that Pothuraju has His own importance, while the other goddesses are now disconnected from the concept of Pothuraju. In Telugu speaking states, we see the 'Cult of Pothuraju' has somehow helped retain the concept. There He is the brother of all the Grama-Devatas. 'The cult of Pothuraju' is now a mere performance, as not many intend to understand or acknowledge the facts of Pothuraju, rather opt to rely on puranic stories.

Chapter 10:

BETAL/ VETAL

10.1 STORIES IN THE LAND OF KONKAN

In the northern parts of Karnataka, from Karwar extending up to Goa, which also includes parts of Maharastra, lies the land of Konkan, where Pothuraju/ Karuppu/ Madan becomes 'BETAL BABA'. There are historical evidences that the 'Kadamba' kings worshipped Betal. Betal is misunderstood by people as 'a corpse hanging upside down' OR 'an illusionary corpse'. Betal is the name given to this deity, to describe His wit, wisdom, valor, fierce and destructive energy. We can see a lot of similarities in the description of this deity with other Grams-Devatas like Karuppu and Madan. Karuppu and Madan, who are the same, but separated later due to stories, difference in their names and the castes who worshipped them. Decades ago, Karuppu/ Madan was offered votives: 'Suruttu' (cigar), sword (aruvaal), alcohol, meat, footwear and black dhoti. Karuppu/ Madan are said to ride on a horse, with a sword or sickle in one hand and bowl/ skull/ mace/ chopped head etc. in the other (which varies according to locations and stories). Buffalo sacrifices were made along with roosters and goats which all had to be preferable black in color. Nowadays, we see that these rules are more flexible based on the availability of these offerings. Recently we see that buffalo sacrifices, foot-wears offered to Karuppu/ Madan is considered impure by most of his devotees. In some places, the concept/ ritual of Karuppu Vettai/ Sudalaimadan Vettai is also skipped (in some temples only).

Surprisingly, these rituals, offerings to Karuppu/ Madan are observed to be similar, in the temples of Betal as well. The offerings to Betal such as footwear, sword, sickle etc. is done by families assembling during the annual visitation to their tutelary deity. But, the buffalo sacrifices, alcohol, meat, cigars, black clothing are now not entertained in Betal temples as the Brahmin priests do not feel comfortable with these methods of appeasing the deity. We also see that the whipping ritual of Pothuraju can also be witnessed during the annual ceremony of Betal temples. Here, in the Konkan regions, He has remained to be a tantric deity, as Vishnumaya in Kerala.

The stories associated to His origin, are not mentioned in any older versions of the puranas, instead these stories could have been sprouted from the creativity of people, and included later when the puranas were augmented. Betal is often seen or compared to "VIKRAM and BETAL", where the concept is totally different. This is a perfect example of how a misunderstanding can become a reason, for a deity to lose its identity and is lost or dodged from the original.

10.1.1 Story 1: Betal, who is considered to be a form of Bhairav, sometimes Veera Bhadhra, in some accounts Siva himself and has idols all over the Konkan region. The idols' height ranges between two to eight feet. Most of his idols are seen holding a sword and skull (bowl). In some places, He is the protector of Durga and in others, he is an independent Deity, just like Karuppu/ Pothuraju.

This village guardian deity of Konkan, Betal – gets His name from the word 'Vetala'. He is a kshetrapal/ guardian deity of a given village or community. He is later included in the puranas when Brahmins: Goud Saraswat, Rajapur Saraswat and a few more Brahmin communities accepted Him as their Tutelary deity. These Brahmin communities included this deity into the puranas around 12th to 13th Century AD. According to Shaivaites, a version of purana states that, Siva and Parvati once were physically intimate and asked Bhairav to guard the door of their sleeping quarters. Parvati then comes out unkempt, Bhairav who was at the door, mocks her, "Women!" and laughs mischievously. He even blocks her from moving, the story further mentions how Bhairav was smitten by her beauty. She immediately curses him to be born a human and do his job right as a guard. Hence Bhairav was born as Betal. Having learnt the situation, Siva consoles Bhairav saying his birth as a human was for a reason and was going to make a huge difference.

In some puranas, ironically Bhairav or Kal-Bhairav is Siva himself (another name for Siva) and according to some sources 'Bhringi-muni' is associated with Vetal, just like the case of various Muneeswaran forms in Tamil Nadu and Karnataka, where a sage becomes a guardian deity. In some texts, Bhairav and Bhringi are born from the spilled semen of Siva, gore and dark complexioned. They were the guards of Siva and Parvati's sleeping quarters.

10.1.2 Story 2: In another version, both Bhringi and Bhairav accidently saw Parvati in a disheveled state, coming out of her bedroom. She cursed the guards to be born with monkey faces, for which they cursed her back, as it was her mistake to walk out of her room in such a state. Hence Siva and Parvati are born on Earth and they give birth to Betal and Bhringi. Betal is later attracted to the celestial nymph 'Urvasi' and fathered a son 'Suvesha'. He also mates with a cow (divine) Kamadhenu and begets a son 'Shringa' and their lineages have continued to exist. This is the belief of the communities who associate themselves with Betal's lineage.

10.1.3 Story 3: Queen 'Taravati' was bathing in a secluded area, where sage 'Kapota' is smitten by her beauty. The seduced sage orders her to satisfy his sexual urge. The scared queen, asks her twin (her younger sister in some versions) who resembles the queen, to take her place. For some reasons, the younger sister agrees to copulate with the sage. It is seen that the queen's sister continued meeting the sage for a while, until one day when she spilled the beans. The furious sage curses the queen Taravati to be raped by a grubby mendicant, a 'Kapalika' and their union would result in two monkey faced sons. She then took a vow on her goddess 'Chandika' to whom she was devoted all her life that, none other than her husband could touch her. The chaste queen, immediately informed the king about the episode. The king builds a skyscraping tower to guard her. Siva and Parvati, understanding the situation, decides to let the canon-effect occur without causing much harm. Parvati enters the body of the queen, staying in the tower, while Siva enters the tower as a Kapalika and rapes her, resulting in the birth of their twin sons, Betal and Bhringi. Later these monkey faced princes are guided by 'Narada' to the ashram of sage Kapota for enlightenment. There these princes are also revealed of their true identity.

10.1.4 Story 4: There is another popular story of Betal, the 'Nagdo Betal'. He is described as a naked dark complexioned man or sometimes a naked man who rides on a horse at night guarding the village, just like the case of Karuppu/ Madan. He arrives with a jingling sound 'Jhal Jhal Jhal', anyone who witnesses His presence deceases. This Betal reached 'Loliem' (Goa) after waging a war and conquering twelve territories. The villagers of Loliem, instantly recognized his valor and strength, wished for Him to stay there as a guardian of their village. 'Nagizan', an old man from the village (in some versions, the Zamindar of the village), dared to request the Betal to stay/ reside in their village. Betal in turn demands for a two-legged, four-legged, ten-legged animal as an offering, finally a foetus, to make the task impossible. Nagizan was a wise man who offered a rooster, buffalo, crab and finally instead of a foetus, he offered 'Areca Nut' (beetle nut) which is a symbol of foetus. He successfully tricked the Betal to stay back in Loliem as the guardian of frontiers. 'Guravs', 'Ghadi', 'Ravals' etc. are the non-Brahmin priests of Nagdo Betal.

Betal – whipping himself & His devotees

Similar to Karuppu/ Madan/ Pothuraju, the origin of Betal too has a version of Him being born to Veera-Bhadhra and Bhadhra-Kali. He too resides in cemeteries and wards off demonic possessions in human. Overall he is a tantric/ vamachara deity. His story has various versions, He also whips his devotees, like Pothuraju, to ward off evil spirits. The story of Mhasoba begins with a note of Mhasoba entering the land of Marathas from the Konkan region, which is Betal himself. He is also worshipped by 'Jats', also in few places of Madhya Pradesh, Rajasthan and Gujarat as 'Gorla'.

Chapter 11:

GORLA

11.1 STORIES IN THE LAND OF GUJARAT & RAJASTHAN

The 'Jat' community and the 'Rajputs' of Rajasthan and Gujarat worship 'Mawli', very similar to the concept of 'Sati-Asaras'/ 'Sapta-Kanyas'/ 'Siri' etc., not many stories are known about 'Gorla & Mawli'. Here Gorla is always seen with His elder sister Mawli and six other sisters whose names vary according to locations and tales. It is said that a king in Rajasthan fathers Mawli and her six sisters, where these six sisters are not of primary importance. The birth of Gorla seems obscure. One day, it is said that Mawli and her six sisters were seated in a palanquin, on their way (destination unknown), due to the supernatural powers that Mawli possessed, disappeared with her sisters and never came back. There are stories, oral traditions, beliefs of Mawli and her sisters who sail in the night sky looking upon the people, who are in distress, in need of help etc. It is said that she even cures physical ailments and disabilities.

Gorla (right most) with 7 sisters, Mawli (seated) in the middle

The newly-weds in Gujarat & Rajasthan, visit Mawli temple to seek her blessing. Here too, not many stories are narrated about Gorla, the brother who accompanies these sisters.

In **Odisha and Madhya Pradesh**, Mawli is a tribal goddess, who wards off evil. She is the elder sister of 'Danteshwari' (Sakti-Peet). She is the tutelary goddess of the 'Kakatiya' kings, who ruled Odisha and Telangana. They called her 'Kakati Devi'.

Chapter 12:

MAHISARURA

12.1 STORIES AND BELIEFS IN CHATTISGARH, JHARKHAND, BENGAL

In the year 2016, a HRD (Human Resources and Development) minister of ruling party in India, churned a heated debate against the tribal, SC, ST and other minority groups. According to her understanding, goddess Durga was a puranic hero or savior while a tribal god like Mahisha had no significance. The minister's comment displayed her lack of knowledge about the vast, diverse culture of our country.

Scholars and experts of scheduled castes and tribes, state that, the idea of idolizing 'Mahisasura' as a benevolent king and an ancestor is spread widely among many tribes and castes in the country.

There are tribes called 'ASUR' in Lehardaga, Latchar, Palamu etc. of Jharkhand and few parts of Bengal. These tribes believe themselves to be descendants of Mahisasura. The 'Santhali' tribe, who is a subdivision of 'Munda' tribe call him 'HUDUR-DURGA' (not to confuse with the Munda tribe of Karnataka). Though the Munda tribe of north and Munda tribe of Karnataka have similar names and beliefs, they do not share any other similarities. On the other hand, 'Toda' tribe and many other tribes (similar to Munda) of Nilgiri in South India, exhibit indifference towards their culture and have converted to Christianity in recent times. These tribes: Munda, Santhal, Toda (Nilgiri), Korku etc. worship Mahisasura or buffaloes. In 'Purulia', an annual fair is held to mark their respect to Mahisasura. He is revered as a king, who valiantly fought against Aryan ideology of subjugating the natives. While in some places, he is a king and in others, a guide or guru.

Mahisasura – the Buffalo King

In Karnataka, Mysuru is named after Mahisasura (Mahisa-Ooru), also in Tamil Sangam Literature 'ERUMAI-NAL-NAADU' which translates to 'the virtuous land where buffalo dwells'. Not only in South India, but tribes residing in Jharkhand, Chhattisgarh and Bengal areas also believe Mahisasura deserves to be worshipped as a deity. These tribes, observe mourning on Navaratri or Dusshera when the entire country celebrates the victory of the goddess over Mahisasura. They sometimes restrict themselves from going out during the ninth and tenth day, scared of something ill may occur to them.

12.1.1 The Story of Asur Tribe:

There is an oral tradition that these tribes narrate. The king Mahisasura was an expert in forging swords, very strong, courageous, stood against the Aryan invasion. The Aryans who called themselves 'Brahmana-Devatas', later in the puranas they put themselves in the place of the Devatas, tried imposing their authority and superiority. Mahisasura kept them at bay. Later Durga is seen inviting him for a drink. Intoxicated Mahisasura drops all his weapons, making the situation easy to kill him. This is the version of Asur tribe's Dusshera.

12.1.2 The Story of Munda Tribe:

Once a male buffalo, wandering in the forests, grazing, finds a girl abandoned. He raises the child as his own. As time goes by, she grows up to be a beautiful girl, whose beauty attracts many. A king falls in love with this girl 'Durga', he sends his men to fetch her, while the male buffalo kills them all with his immense strength. The king later cages him and takes the girl away, later the buffalo dies of sorrow. In some versions, the king slays the buffalo and marries the girl.

12.1.3 The Story of Santhali Tribe:

Here, Mahisasura is addressed as Durga/ Durgamasura. Apparently, the puranas speak of Durgamasura as a different Asur king. The Aryan forces, when invaded India, they found really difficult to fit in. They lacked strength and possession over the land, king Durga being the reason. They ploy against king Durga, where, an accord marriage is arranged as a mark of peace between the Aryans and king Durga. A Brahmin girl 'Devi' is chosen, whose enchanting beauty could blind king Durga. They both get married and she actually falls in love with him eventually. One day, the Aryans visit king Durga, and explain him about their custom to meet their daughter with the goodies they had brought with them. They meet her in private and force her to kill the king, for the sake of their community. She refuses to do so. They finally plead her to arrange a meeting with the king, but the condition being, both parties unarmed. She agrees to it and it is seen that the Aryans betray by carrying weapons with them. They get Durga intoxicated, kill him brutally and hide his corpse. His subjects are immediately informed about his absence. His worried subjects wander, singing songs about him, hoping to find their beloved king soon. Meanwhile, the Aryans covet the lands through Devi, king Durga's wife and she becomes Durga herself, as a mark of transfer in power.

In these narrations, we see that Mahisasura could have been a tribal king, with buffalo as his totem or emblem. As the Mahisasura culture was spread so vast, we see many communities in many parts of the country have struggled to keep the culture intact. Some have given up their identity, for the fear of being discriminated as inferior. Also, there are some, who are not ready to accept that, their deity is nothing but a name changed version of Mahisasura, because the puranas have portrayed him as evil and pervert. Instead, they are more comfortable in stories that are in no way related to their deities. The puranic contamination discriminates these characters as good and bad deities. *The tribal stories/ folklores at every point are argued to lack logic, while the magical versions of the puranas seem more practical to the people surprisingly.*

Buffaloes have been considered to be a symbol of strength and prosperity by many cultures. In the North-East part of India, we see that tribes like 'Rongmei', 'Angami', 'Adi' etc. share the same opinion. They decorate their houses with paintings of Buffalo heads, buffalo skulls and 'Tengka' designs as a symbol of abundance. They sacrifice Bisons/ Buffaloes at their village festivities, the members of the tribe assemble to receive their share of meat, as a gesture of togetherness.

Chapter 13:

BHAIRAV, the smuggled concept of Pothuraju?

The altered identity of Pothuraju is not new, He becomes Bhairav in some places, whereas Veera Bhadhra in few, he becomes a hero in folklores, a villain in the puranas. When the (puranas) Aryans could not impose their ideas on a deity, they split a character in two, where one becomes the villain and another becomes a savior. There are too many examples as such.

In sixteenth to seventeenth century, during the rule of 'MALLA Dynasty', King Pratap Malla was informed about a Bhairav statue that was found in the paddy fields of Katmandu, Nepal. This statue was carved out of a single stone, was ferocious and majestic. King Pratap Malla, then installed this statue in Darbar Square, Katmandu. Bhairav was designated as the guardian of Nepal (Malla Kingdom) ever since. Later it is seen that many other Bhairav temples were erected by the royal families around the same time period. The Kal-Bhairav in Darbar Square is considered to be 'Ruru-Bhairav', one of the eight forms of Bhairav. Here's a tricky part, this Bhairav is offered buffalo heads as an offering, also the meat. No any other surviving temples of Bhairav in India, have the practice of buffalo sacrifices. Bhairav is often seen as one of those deities, whom Aryans used as a tool of conversion, of bloody sacrifices made by tribes, to 'Satvik' methods. Though He makes His entry in the later version of puranas, gains popularity faster, as His cult already existed in huge numbers accepted His new name and version faster. In Nepal, He is seen as the companion of 'Asta-Maatrikas' (an extended version of Sapta-Maatrikas/ seven-sister concept, Pratyangira being the additional eighth goddess). These eight goddesses are assigned eight different forms of Bhairavs as a consort/ guardian. This very concept exists in the Buddhist pantheon also. During the festivities of Bhairav in Nepal, the royal priest plays the part of an oracle or the voice of Bhairav, predicting the future of the royals and all of Nepal.

13.1 THE STORY IN NEPAL:

Apart from being treated as a divine entity, it is said that He was born a human (king) once. The king of Virata, the war Lord Bhairav himself. These descriptions are very similar to 'Pothiraja' mentioned in the Tamil land. In Tamil Nadu, the 'VILLUPATU' performers sing praises of Pothiraja, 'VEERA VANNIYAN' – war lord, 'VIRATA DESATTU MANNAN' – king of Virata. He who holds a slayed head and a guardian of goddesses, shows the similarity between Pothiraja and Bhairav of Nepal. He is praised as 'the sword forger', He who grants the sword and other divine weapons to kings, granting them victory, like in the Asur tribe version of story.

According to the story, Kal-Bhairav of Nepal was born in a royal family of Virata kingdom, where He decapitates 'Indra', the king of Devatas, (Indra in another version was the king's purohit). He is said to have reincarnated as a low caste dancer. Every pushkar (i.e., 12 years) a sword that was newly forged by Bhairav himself/ blessed by Bhairav in some accounts, is exchanged with the previous one, for the king of Nepal.

This ceremony commences every once in twelve years where the new sword of Bhairav is replaced with the king's old sword, assuring victory to the king. This ritual is carried out by Buddhist-Brahmins called 'Vajra-Acharyas'. These are the elite class Buddhist Brahmins of Nepal. These were the priests who carried the concept of Bhairav to Nakoda, Rajasthan. This 'Nakoda-Bhairav' was later adopted by the Jains.

Chapter 14:

YAMANTAKA

During the formation of 'Mahayana' philosophy in Buddhism, the Buddhist Brahmin cult introduced the idea of 'Bhairav' or 'the wrathful Siva', he was incorporated into the tantric 'Vajrayana'. Though 'Hinayana' philosophy does not entertain idol worship or the existence of divine, 'Mahayana', which was the later outcome of Buddhism, outnumbered the Hinayana sect replacing the original idea of 'Bodhisatva'. In the Vajrayana Buddhism, the idea of 'Yamantaka' is purely tantric, he who defies death. Yamantaka is the deity who eradicates ignorance. The name 'Yamantaka' (Yama-Death, Antaka-Destroyer) may have been the idea of 'Kalantaka' – a Hindu puranic god/ form of Siva. He is considered to be one of the 24 forms of Bhairav ('Manjusri' concept). He is often confused with 'Yama' – 'the Lord of Death', as he rides on an Indian water buffalo, but as the name suggests he defies Yama or the conqueror of Yama.

Yamantaka has his own pantheon in Vajrayana Buddhism. The story of Yamantaka defers slightly when compared to Hindu puranas. In the puranas, Bhairav/ Kal-Bhairav defeats Yama for the sake of 'Markhandeya', whereas, in Buddhism, Yamantaka conquers Yama because of interrupting the flow of Karma (untimely death). Yama turned arrogant as he felt that he could take the lives of anyone at any point he wished, even before their Karmic-Cleanse, thus challenging the pre-determined algorithm of the Universe. Bhairav/ Yamantaka defeats Yama and restores balance. He is considered more powerful when worshipped with his consort 'Vajra-Vetali' (as illusionary corpse), making him 'Vajra-Bhairav'/ 'Vajra-Betal'. Here the term 'Vajra' is to brief the preeminence of a deity in Buddhism. He is often seen with a buffalo face, riding a buffalo. This idea of Yamantaka has travelled to every country Buddhism spread, Vietnam, China, Tibet, Japan, Indonesia etc. He stays in the highest tier of tantric Buddhism, in a sexual embrace with Vajra-Vetali (Yab-Yum). This buffalo-headed deity represents wisdom and compassion, often explained to be surrounded by ghosts and 'Vetalas', purely tantric and above all the 'mantras'. Here, we see that, the earlier versions of Hinduism may have influenced the Mahayana, where the buffalo-headed deity, when absorbed into Buddhism, is in his least altered form.

The later versions of Bhairav (a.k.a. Pothuraju) in Hinduism may have gained a human face due to various influences. His sexual embrace or coitus pose with the goddess may have its roots from the pre-vedic ideologies of the goddess's relationship with the buffalo king (like in the cases: Uramma, Marikambe, Dhyamayi etc.).

In the Indus Valley Civilization, 'Mohenjadaro', etched seals were obtained and through studies, it was found that buffaloes were sacrificed as a ritual to either a god/ deity or a person who wore buffalo horns, who could have been a shaman/ oracle/ priest onto whom the divine would descend. These tantric practices of sacrificing buffaloes, fowls, goats dates back to 1800 to 1000 BCE.

EPILOGUE

What to Comprehend?

This is an honest attempt, based on research and studies contributed by many, apart from my interest. We put these topics in front of you, to culminate.

All these deities (pre-vedic gods) are still a topic of discussion as their origins are uncertain. This paved way for them to blend with the characters in puranas that were introduced in the later period of history.

Does all these pre-vedic deities share similarities or are these deities the same which may have taken myriad forms and stories, because of the diverse Indian diaspora? We are trying to trace the origin and the journey of the 'buffalo king' that has crossed boundaries and has survived influences.

The deities: Betal, Mhasoba, Pothuraju, Karuppu, Sudalai Madan, Madan, Tala-Vai-Madan (still speculative), Maisonday, Mahisasura of South are in a way well connected through similar rituals, yet distinct. The rituals like: buffalo sacrifices are now suppressed, but the other rituals are kept intact like: whipping (Saattai-Adi), 'Perambadi', 'Flambeau March', 'Vettai' (hunt), patrolling the village during the nights, bibulous of animal blood etc. The offerings are also common among these, while some of these offerings are being altered or stopped due to various reasons, such as alcohol, cigars, footwear, swords, sickles, Silambu etc. However, are all these similarities enough to conclude that these different deities are the same by origin?

At this point, we have to question ourselves, does it mean that associating these deities with puranic characters and making room for them in the puranas make them superior? Are we not proud of our origin? Rather trade the deity's originality, assuming to have upgraded their positions? The puranas were composed to market the Bhakti Movement, it was made to sound magical, to attract the attention of the crowd.

The folklores later adopted these methods of magical interpretations due to the fear of losing their importance, yet were left unnoticed.

The puranas were written around 3rd century and were constantly altered and were augmented with new episodes, up to 10th century, with various versions. Even the puranas have different versions (stories) of any given deity. It's proven to be inconsistent in many accounts. But we chose to rely on them and wedge the pre-vedic deities into them and consider it as a part of upgrading. Not being proud of our deities who have existed even before the Vedic and puranic periods, we have succumbed ourselves along with our deities and culture to the Aryan imposition. Constantly degrading these pre-vedic deities, with false assumptions of upgrading them, according to Aryan standards.

Keep aside the puranas, all the magic, miracles, where does it leave these deities then? Now explain the origin of these deities. Aren't we stuck in an 'impasse'? That's how much we have lost our identity and our culture uprooted.

We are the reason for this impact on our pre-vedic deities, who are now the second class deities, portrayed to serve or guard the Aryan Gods.

9 789334 226553

Printed at Repro India Ltd.